# COGNITIVE BEHAVIORAL THERAPY

*How to Break Free from Depression, Anxiety, Anger and Negative Thoughts - Develop Resilience without Resorting to Harmful Medication*

## Wallace Foulds

# Text Copyright © 2018 Wallace Foulds



## Legal & Disclaimer

provided by this guide. This disclaimer applies to any damages or injury caused by the use and application, whether directly or indirectly, of any advice or information presented, whether for breach of contract, tort, negligence, personal injury, criminal intent, or under any other cause of action.

You agree to accept all risks of using the information presented inside this book. You need to consult a professional medical practitioner in order to ensure you are both able and healthy enough to participate in this program.

# Table of Contents


Introduction ...........................................1

What is the subconscious mind? ...........................5

What is the conscious mind? ..............................11

What is Cognitive Behavioral Therapy? .....................17

Identifying the Problem ..................................29

Dismantling Toxic Thoughts ...............................41

How to Refocus and Retrain Your Awareness ................55

Reaching Forward to the Things Ahead .....................67

Ten Attitudes That Promote a Healthy Mind ................77

Conclusion ..............................................89

# Introduction

**M**ost people did not believe me when I tell them that I suffered from severe depression, anxiety, anger issues and general negative thinking six years ago. Although I had a stable and well-paid job back then as a Research Associate, my personal and workplace relationships were adversely affected by my mental health. I couldn't understand what had happened to me. I had taken every medication possible, seen counsellors and psychiatrists and nothing seemed to work. One day, I randomly stumbled across an article about the benefits of Cognitive Behavioral Therapy (CBT). I had tried everything else, so I thought I might as well try this too, I was desperate to get off medication because of the terrible side effects I was experiencing. Well, here I am, six years later, drug free and most importantly free from mental illness. I beat it with Cognitive Behavioral Therapy!

I saw a psychologist for a few years who meticulously walked me through the steps of CBT until I felt confident enough to go it alone. What I can tell you is that CBT works if you stick to it. The problem with non-medicinal therapy is that it doesn't work straight away, it took months before I began to experience a noticeable different to my psychological well-being. This is where most people give up. Unfortunately, we live in a microwave society, just pop it in and out it comes ready in two minutes! Life doesn't work like that, if you are going to achieve anything worthwhile, you are going to have to put in some serious effort.

I can't tell you about anything else other than what worked for me, and because it worked, I am passionate about seeing other people set free from mental illness so that they can live the life of wholeness and abundance that they deserve.

This book provides you with a comprehensive introduction to the theory and application of Cognitive Behavioral Therapy techniques. Please bear in mind that there is more to CBT than what I have documented, but space restrictions won't allow me to go into more detail. However, what you have is enough to get you started and lead you in the right direction.

I believe that all the CBT principles outlined in this book can help you regardless of whether your symptoms are mild or severe. When I was first introduced to some of the CBT techniques that I have mentioned, I must admit that I was a bit sceptical, but as I have stated, they worked, and they continue to work. In fact, they are extremely powerful. Therefore, I am asking that you remain open-minded as you go through this book.

I wish you every success in your journey to mental freedom!

# What is the subconscious mind?

Before we can even start talking about Cognitive Behavioral Therapy, you have to understand the mind. CBT deals with the mind and the mind only, before you go ahead with any therapy session your psychologist will explain how your mind works to help you to gain a better understanding of yourself.

When the word 'subconscious' is mentioned, it is often misjudged as something spooky. The majority of people are completely ignorant of how their subconscious mind works. Once you realize what a powerful tool it is, you will immediately start to use it to your advantage.

You can compare the subconscious mind to a large memory bank. It contains an unlimited capacity to store every experience that you have had in your life. Are you aware that by the time you are 21 years of age you have already stored the equivalent of the entire contents of the Encyclopaedia

Britannica one hundred times over in your subconscious mind!

When older people are hypnotized, they have the ability to remember with clarity things that they experienced during their childhood years. Your subconscious mind is in perfect health, it is your conscious mind that is the problem.

The purpose of your subconscious mind is to retrieve and store information. Its role is to make sure that your actions line up with the way you have been programmed. Everything you say and do fits a consistent pattern that lines up with your unique concept of self. Your subconscious mind will ensure that this happens.

This is one of the main reasons why doing things such as reciting inspirational quotes work so well for people who are determined to change the way they think. When your thoughts are focused on things that motivate you, the subconscious mind will begin to establish a positive pattern in the way you think and view life.

Your subconscious mind doesn't do anything independently, it is not subjective. It does one thing, and that is to obey the commands that it receives from the conscious mind. Think about it this way, your conscious mind is the gardener that plants seeds. Your conscious mind is the fertile soil or the garden where the seeds grow. I hope you are learning to understand why positive thinking is so important? Your conscious thoughts are constantly providing your unconscious mind with the direction in which to steer your life. There is no escape from this reality.

Your subconscious mind doesn't question anything, it isn't going to tell your conscious mind to stop sending thoughts. It works nonstop to ensure that your behavior lines up with your emotionalized desires, hopes and thoughts. It will either grow weeds or flowers in the garden of your life. The only person who can decide what it grows is you.

Your subconscious mind contains something referred to as a 'homeostatic impulse.' This makes sure that your body temperature remains at 98.6 degrees F, it also regulates your heart beat and establishes a regular breathing pattern. The body was created to function in complete harmony, the automatic nervous system makes sure that the billions of cells in your body are perfectly balanced in order to do this.

Homeostasis encourages the conscious mind to keep you acting and thinking in a way that is consistent with the things that you have said and done in the past. Your behavioral and thinking habits are all housed in your subconscious mind. It has kept a memory of everything that you are comfortable doing and it works to keep you in them.

Whenever you try and do something different or new, or change an established pattern of behavior, your subconscious mind will make you feel physically and emotionally uncomfortable. The sense of discomfort and fear are cerebral signs that your subconscious has been activated. Before you even notice these feelings, your subconscious mind has been functioning to establish those patterns of behavior.

The reason why people find it so difficult to break bad habits is because they are committed to negative behavior patterns. However, once you learn to intentionally establish new patterns of behavior, you will formulate new habits that will shift your comfort zone and your subconscious will adapt to it.

Every time you try something new you will feel your subconscious mind dragging you back into the zone that you are most comfortable. The mere thought of doing something that you are not familiar with will make you feel uneasy and tense.

Extremely successful people are always stretching themselves outside of their comfort zone. They are very aware of how easy it is to become comfortable in a particular area. They know that complacency is the enemy to success.

If you are going to grow and successfully break out of your comfort zone, you are going to have to embrace the uncomfortable feelings that come along with it. You are not going to succeed the first few times you try, and this is why the majority of people give up because they don't see immediate results. You have to understand that whatever negative habits you have, whether it's your thought life or your behavioral patterns, they didn't just develop overnight, you have cultivated them since the day you were born.

As you will learn, the main aim of Cognitive Behavioral Therapy is to reprogram your subconscious mind; it will train your brain to come into alignment with your true desires, life goals and dreams. Before we get to Cognitive Behavioral Therapy, let's take a look at how the conscious mind works.

# What is the conscious mind?

The conscious mind is referred to as the thinking mind, or the objective mind. It is only capable of holding one thought at a time. The mind has got four main functions.

**1: Analyze Incoming Information:** Every day we receive information through either feeling, touch, taste, smell, sound and sight. The conscious mind is always categorizing and observing what is going on around you. For example, let's say you are walking along the street and you decide to cross the road, as you go to step out you hear the loud roar of a car engine. You turn around straight away to find out what direction the car is coming from. This is the first function of the conscious mind.

**2: Comparison:** The information that you have recorded then travels to the subconscious mind to determine whether it has is similar to any of the other previously stored experiences and information with moving cars. If the car is travelling at 20 mph and it is still a block away, the memories in your subconscious mind will communicate a message to your conscious mind that there is no immediate danger and you can keep walking.

If the car is coming towards you at 70 mph, and it is only 200 yards away, your subconscious mind will communicate a message of danger to your conscious mind, and you will act accordingly by choosing not to step out into the road.

**3: Analysis:** Before you make a decision (which is the fourth function of the mind) you have to analyze and evaluate the information. Your conscious mind works in the same way as a binary computer, it performs two major functions. It accepts or rejects information when you are making decisions and choices. As mentioned earlier, it can only handle single thought. These are either yes or no, or positive or negative. This is the main reason why individuals who are working towards a lifestyle of positive thinking read uplifting quotes. We have one track minds that are only capable of entertaining one thought at a time. If we are continuously thinking positive, it cancels out negative thinking.

Positive affirmations are also extremely helpful for occupying our brains with empowering and pleasant thoughts. Visualization is also a very powerful tool.

**4: Decision:** So when you hear the car coming towards you, because your subconscious mind contains stored knowledge of the speed of moving vehicles, when you analyze the information and it tell you that you are in danger, a decision is required. The first question you are going to ask yourself is, "Do I move out of the way? Yes or no?"

If the answer is yes, you will then ask yourself something like, "Do I jump forwards? Yes or no?" If there is oncoming traffic and the answer is "no", you will then ask yourself "if you should jump backwards? Yes or no?" If the answer is "yes," this message is immediately transmitted to your subconscious mind, and your entire body jumps backwards. This all sounds like a long and complicated process, but it isn't, this will all take place within less than a second.

You are currently using your conscious mind to read and to process these words. You are repeating the words in your mind as you read the information on this page. As you start to gain understanding from the text, you start thinking about how it relates to you and your current situation. The conscious mind is logical, sequential and linear, it wants everything to make sense, and if it doesn't, it will kick out the information and move onto something else that it finds easier to process. However, the subconscious mind has still stored the information regardless of whether you have understood it or not.

If all you hear as a child are words of abuse, they are stored in your subconscious mind, and it is these words that steer the course of your life. Have you ever wondered why there are some people who jump from one abusive relationship to another? To the outsider looking in, this behavior makes no sense, but to the subconscious mind, it makes perfect sense, because this is how it has been programmed. A child who was raised in an abusive environment, whether they experienced the abuse themselves, or witnessed it is more likely to end up in an abusive relationship as an adult.

During therapy, mentally ill patients who suffer from conditions such as depression and anxiety will often find that their problems are due to some type of abuse that they have suffered in life, whether in childhood or adult years. For example, in a study published in the American Journal of Psychiatry, researchers found that teenagers and young adults who had experienced bullying, witnessed domestic violence, or experienced abuse as a child had higher levels of hostility, anxiety and depression. Previous studies have also found that socially unhealthy environments can lead to brain impairment in children.

The bottom line is that words stick, and they stick in the subconscious mind; therefore, it is essential that reprogramming takes place so that the individual can set themselves free from patterns of negative behavior. This is where Cognitive Behavioral Therapy comes into the picture.

# What is Cognitive Behavioral Therapy?

Cognitive behavioral therapy helps people to find a new and better way of thinking and dealing with their problems. As you go through this chapter and the rest of this book, you will find that the majority of what you will learn appear like common sense practices. However, as you have read about the subconscious mind, when certain beliefs and behaviors have been ingrained, even the simplest new habits can be impossible to adapt to. CBT will help you to maximize your common sense abilities, and help you to replace unhealthy behaviors and practices with new healthy habits that will help you to overcome mental illnesses such as depression, anxiety, negative thinking and anger.

## Why CBT is a Reliable Method

The benefits of Cognitive Behavioral Therapy have been researched more extensively than any other psychotherapeutic approach. Over recent years, CBT has gained a reputation as a highly effective treatment. A number of studies have found that CBT can treats conditions such as anxiety and depression better than medication. Scientists are continuing to research Cognitive Behavioral Therapy, this has led to more being discovered in terms of the treatments that are most beneficial for different people and different conditions.

Research has found that people who have CBT for problems such as depression and anxiety, remain well for longer periods of time, they also relapse far less than patients who only take medication to treat their condition. These results are likely due to the fact that CBT isn't just bound to a doctor's office or taking a pill. Patients are given a lot of educational material which they can take home and continue their treatment independently if they wish.

An increasing number of psychiatrists and physicians are referring their patients for Cognitive Behavioral Therapy to help them to defeat problems such as:

- Anxiety

- Addiction

- Anger

- Body dysmorphic disorder

- Chronic pain

- Chronic fatigue syndrome

- Depression

- Eating disorders

- Obsessive compulsive disorders

- Personality disorder

- Panic disorder

- Post traumatic stress disorder

- Phobias

- Psychotic disorders

- Relationship problems

- Social phobias

This book will only cover a few of the conditions mentioned; however, the techniques and skills discussed can be applied to the majority of psychological problems.

COGNITIVE BEHAVIORAL THERAPY

## What is Cognitive Behavioral Therapy?

As previously mentioned, Cognitive Behavioral Therapy is a form of psychotherapy that is used to assist people in overcoming their emotional problems.

- **Cognitive:** Refers to a mental process such as thinking, it is related to everything that takes place in the mind such as attention, thoughts, images, memories and dreams.

- **Behavior:** Is related to the way you behave. This includes your problem solving techniques, the things you say, the things you avoid and the way you act in general. Behavior is related to both inaction and action, for example, refraining from speech instead of saying what you really want to is still viewed as a behavior even though you are making an effort not to do something.

- **Therapy:** This is a term used to describe a systematic approach to dealing with physical or mental problems.

The main thread that runs throughout Cognitive Behavioral Therapy is that you feel the way you think. Therefore, the belief system of CBT is that you can live a happy and productive life if you your thinking is healthy.

## Combining Behavior, Philosophy And Science

One of the reasons why CBT is so powerful is that it combines behavioral, philosophical and scientific aspects into one comprehensive method of overcoming and understanding psychological problems.

- **Scientific:** CBT has been developed and tested through numerous scientific studies, it also encourages its patients to take on the characteristics of a scientist. For example, a CBT patient might develop the ability to treat their thoughts as theories that should be tested instead of reality. In science, this is referred to as a hypothesis.

- **Philosophical:** CBT acknowledges the fact that people hold beliefs and values about themselves, other people, and the world. One of the main aims of CBT is to assist people in developing self-helping, non-extreme and flexible beliefs that help them to face the reality in which they are living and achieve their goals.

Cognitive Behavioral Therapy encourages you to understand that your beliefs or thinking lies somewhere between the event, your actions and the way you feel. The meaning that you place on an event, your beliefs and your thoughts produce your behavioral and emotional responses.

So Cognitive Behavioral Therapy would say that your boyfriend does not make you upset. Rather, your boyfriend behaves in a way that you don't like. You then assign a meaning to this behaviour, such as, "He is doing this on purpose to hurt me." Therefore, you are the one who is responsible for how you feel.

The A,B,C formula, is used in CBT to help patients make sense of their emotional problems.

- **A** equals *activating or actual event*

- **B** equals *beliefs and meanings* related to the event

- **C** equals *consequence* of your emotions and behaviour

**Understanding The Meanings Attached to Events**

Whatever meaning you attach to an event will influence the emotional response that you have to that event. Events that you feel are positive will lead to you attaching feelings of excitement or happiness to it. Negative events lead you to attach feelings of sadness or anxiety to it.

However, there is the possibility that you can attach the wrong meaning to an event. Your thought process can lead you to attach extreme meanings to an event which can leave you feeling distressed. Here is a scenario for you to think about:

Jackie is introduced to a man called Tim on a night out by one of her friends. After a long conversation, they decide that they like each other and exchange numbers. They spend a few weeks talking on the phone, and Tim asks Jackie out on a date. They go out and have a fantastic time and Jackie is expecting Tim to ask her out on a second date. She hasn't heard from him in a few weeks, and so Jackie gets depressed. The fact that Tim didn't ask Jackie out again contributes to her feeling upset. But the real reason she feels depressed is because of the meaning that she has attached to the event. Jackie feels as if Tim has rejected her, which confirms the beliefs that she has about herself that she is unattractive, old, and will remain single for the rest of her life.

Jackie's story is a simple example of how attaching negative meanings to an event can lead to a situation becoming extremely distressing. She could have chosen to believe that they just weren't right for each other, and continued to date until she found the right one.

You can help yourself to work out whether or not the meanings you are giving to events are causing you unnecessary stress by answering the following questions:

- **Is the meaning I am giving to this event unnecessarily extreme?**

- **Am I making broad conclusions about my life because of one event?**

- **Does the meaning I have assigned to this event lead me to feel better or worse about myself?**

If you answer yes to the majority of these questions, then you are probably giving yourself unnecessary stress about a particular event. This is not to say that there is no such thing as a negative event, as we know there are plenty. However, the negative event becomes a problem when you allow it to define you. In later chapters you learn how to correct these negative thinking patterns.

**Your Behavior**

Your thoughts and feelings determine your behaviour. If you feel depressed you are likely to isolate yourself and withdraw from people. If you are anxious, you will avoid situations that you find dangerous or threatening. There are many ways that your behaviors can become problematic, these include:

- **Self Destructive Behaviors:** Using drugs or excessive drinking to eliminate anxiety can lead to physical damage.

- **Isolating behaviors:** Avoiding seeing friends and family or staying in bed all day will increase feelings of isolation and keep you feeling depressed.

- **Avoidance behaviors:** Avoiding situations that you feel are threatening will rob you of the chance to overcome your fears.

**How to Use The ABC Formula**

I mentioned the ABC formula earlier on; here is a quick reminder of it:

**A – Activating Event:** This refers to either a real event that has taken place, a future even that s about to take place, or an event that is taking place in your mind such as a dream, a memory or an image. The activating event is what is known as the trigger.

**B – Beliefs:** Your beliefs include the way you think about a situation, the demands and rules that you place on yourself and the people around you, and the meanings that you attach to events.

**C – Consequences:** These include the physical sensations and feelings that accompany your emotions.

The ABC technique is an effective tool used during Cognitive Behavioral Therapy. It is carried out in a written format so that the patient is able to make a distinction between their thoughts, feelings and behaviors and the event that triggers them. If you suffer from anxiety, the ABC formula is going to look something like this:

**A:** You imagine that you are doing really badly in an interview.

**B:** You believe that you have to do well in the interview or it will validate your belief that you are a failure.

**C:** You start to feel anxious because of your beliefs, and so you decide to use alcohol to calm you down.

You can create your own ABC formula and use it with the above example to guide you when you are filling it out. You need to make sure that you develop a really clear ABC of your problem, so that you can step back and evaluate your thought process in order for you to be able to work at changing it.

**The Main Characteristics of CBT**

Due to space restrictions, it is impossible to go into detail about each individual characteristic of Cognitive Behavioral Therapy. However, below is a quick reference list of the main characteristics:

- Places emphasis on the role that the personal meanings you attach to events play on your emotional response to a situation.

- Came about as the result of extensive scientific research.

- The focus is on how you are maintaining your problems as opposed to finding the root of the problem.

- Offers practical tools and advice on how to overcome common emotional problems.

- Believes that you can change the way a person thinks by implementing new ideas and strategies.

- Looks at your past history to determine how it is affecting the way you think and behave.

- Reveals how some of the strategies you use to cope with emotional problems are not helping but contributing to them.

- Works at normalizing your emotions, thoughts and physical sensations instead of trying to persuade you that there is a hidden problem behind them.

# Identifying the Problem

So let me ask you a question, when was the last time you thought about what you were thinking about? You have probably answered that you are not sure, because the bottom line is that this is not an activity that you indulge in. Not to worry, you are no different than the rest of the world. However, this is a practice that you need to cultivate.

One of the dominant messages of Cognitive Behavioral Therapy is that your thoughts, beliefs and attitudes play an important role in the way you feel and interpret the world around you. So if you are feeling sad, anxious or depressed, there is a high likelihood that your thinking is negative. Of course, you don't aim to think negatively, and you are probably not aware that you do.

Thinking negative thoughts is something that the majority of us do every once in a while. You can compare this to the way a computer virus prevents a computer from doing what it needs to do. So does negative thinking, it prevents you from analyzing your experiences in the right way. Bad thinking will lead you to assume the worst and jump to conclusions. This doesn't sound very promising, but the good news is that there is a way out.

Have you ever been through an embarrassing situation, and at the time you thought it was the worst experience of your life. Years later you looked back on it, realized how ridiculous it was and laughed? Well why didn't you laugh when it happened back then? The reason is because of the way that you thought about it at that time.

In Cognitive Behavioral Therapy, cognitive distortions mean that the way you are thinking about a situation doesn't line up with what is actually going on. A therapist would work with you to identify negative thinking patterns so that you can change them. When you learn how to recognize distorted thinking, you are able to question such thoughts, challenge them and then replace them with thoughts that are more realistic and reasonable.

Cognitive distortions can propel you into a downward spiral of decline that can make you feel as if there is no escape. It creates a negative loop that eventually affects your behavior. I refer to cognitive distortions as a loop because you just continue to go around and around in the same direction. The way you think affects the way you feel, and the way you feel affects your behaviour. The way you behave then triggers more negative thinking, and the cycle begins all over again.

For example, thoughts such as "I don't think anyone likes me," will cause you to feel self-conscious and anxious when you are around people. This will cause you to start having a physical reaction such as an accelerated heart rate and sweaty palms. This then causes you to isolate yourself from people, which results in you feeling alienated. This then leads you to think that there is definitely something wrong with you if you are constantly alone, and the cycle continues.

Before you can change the way you think, you have to recognize the negative thoughts that you are processing. There are some cognitive distortions that are more common than others, here are ten of them.

## 1: Ought's and Shoulds

People that think in 'ought's' and 'shoulds' find it impossible to see things through any other lenses apart from their own. They think that everyone 'should' be or 'ought' to be a certain way, and if not, they feel resentment, disappointment, frustration and anger.

## 2: The Act of Catastrophizing

Catastrophizing is when an insignificant minor event causes us to imagine all sorts of terrible disasters as a result of it. For example:

- You trip up in front of the girl that you like. Once you have managed to peel yourself off the floor, you run home and can't sleep because you now believe that the girl that you like thinks you are a total idiot because you fell over.

- You've met a guy and he's asked you out on a date. You arrive at the location where you have arranged to meet but he isn't there yet. After waiting for 15 minutes you decide to call him but his phone is off. You immediately assume that he was just playing games with you all along, and he's probably spying on you and laughing with a friend somewhere.

- Your friend invites her new boyfriend out to dinner with you guys. You ask him how he is doing, but he doesn't hear you. You ask again, and he still doesn't hear you. You immediately jump to the conclusion that he is purposefully ignoring you because he wants break your friendship up so that he won't have to share his girlfriend with you.

Catastrophizing leads people to view the most innocent situations as complete disasters. A late arrival translates into a car accident, a small disagreement into abandonment and rejection. Eliminate catastrophic thinking by seeing it for what it is, and at the core of it, all you are dealing with is negative thinking. When you realize that you are thinking of the worst possible scenario, put the following strategies into practice:

- Even if the girl you like did see you trip over, how do you know that she wasn't sympathetic. She might not have found it funny at all, you probably didn't even see her laughing. Surely you are not the only person in the world who has ever tripped up in front of the person they are interested in dating. You also need to understand that people are far too self centred to be thinking about one embarrassing moment, chances are they are too busy thinking about their own short falls.

- Think about less extreme explanations. Could your date have lost his phone? Which meant that he has lost your number, and a family emergency came up which is why he was unable to meet you? Don't be so caught up in extreme emotions because he might contact you and give you a perfectly valid explanation for why he couldn't make it.

- What evidence do you have that suggests that your friend's new boyfriend is plotting to ruin your friendship? Since this is the first time you have met him, is it wise to jump to such extreme conclusions so early?

- Is there anything you can do to cope with the situation? Going out on a few dates might help you to get over tripping over in front of the person that you like. If you feel as if a situation has lead to a damaged relationship, you can make attempts to fix it or you can find another relationship.

The bottom line is that no matter how much of a disaster you create in your mind, there is not much chance that the world is going to end because of it. Even if the worst case scenario does come to pass, is it going to kill you? Probably not, you are more capable of surviving painful and embarrassing events than you give yourself credit for.

### 3: Personalisation

An individual who personalizes everything believes that they are to blame for every negative event that takes place.

Personalization is also referred to as 'The mother of guilt' due to the feelings of inadequacy, shame and guilt that it leads to. For example, your dog hurt his foot when you were out. Even though you were not there at the time, you feel as if it was your fault, and you start to think thoughts like, "I should never have gone out." Or "Maybe I stepped on his foot by accident when I came home." Despite the fact that these thoughts are totally unrealistic, you still feel justified in thinking them.

## 4: Emotional Reasoning

This is when we make the assumption that the way we feel is factual despite the evidence that we are presented with. The premise is, that because you feel it, it has to be true. Such thoughts can spark self fulfilling prophecies, in other words, you the way you think ends up becoming your reality. For example, if you think that you are stupid and ugly, your thoughts will lead you to believe that there is no point in trying to look nice because you are ugly anyway. This will then lead you to stop buying new clothes and grooming yourself. Now that you have stopped looking after yourself, you actually do look ugly. Since you believe that you are stupid, there isn't any point in you studying for your exams because you are going to fail anyway. Since you didn't study for your exams, you end up failing. Your thoughts have now become your reality, and you really are ugly and stupid!

## 5: Jumping to Conclusions

A person who jumps to conclusions will often misinterpret information and form a conclusion that doesn't line up with the facts, and there is no evidence to back what they are thinking. People who jump to conclusions will often assume that they know what other people are thinking, or they predict what other peoples intentions are towards them.

For example, you go to a party wearing an outfit that you are not really too fond of because you don't have anything else to wear. When you see people laughing, you assume that that they are laughing at you, even though you haven't heard them mention anything about your outfit.

## 6: All or Nothing Thinking

All or nothing thinking leads to extreme behaviors or emotions. There is no middle ground with this type of thinking. People either hate you or they love you, something is either a disaster or its perfect. You are either totally to blame or free of all responsibility. Does any of this sound sensible? I hope you have answered no?

Depressed, anxious, negative and angry people have a tendency to think in absolutes, despite the fact that the majority of life events are never absolutely perfect or completely disastrous.

## 7: Overgeneralization

People who over generalize when they think will view one bad experience as evidence that nothing will ever go right in their life. For example, you go to a job interview but you don't get the job. This one rejection leads you to think that you will never get a job. Or, you go on a date that doesn't quite turn out as planned; therefore, you decide that you are going to be single for the rest of your life.

## 8: Disqualifying The Positive

People who disqualify the positive refuse to accept anything positive in their lives. For example, a friend says "You look really nice today," your immediate thought is, "She is lying." Or you cook dinner for your friend, and he tells you that you've done a good job. Your immediate thought is he's only saying that because he wants something.

## 9: Mental Filter

This type of thinking is when you only focus on the negative aspects of a situation. The event may have been largely positive, but you choose to ignore this. For example, you gave a talk at work, 98 percent of your colleagues gave you positive feedback. Instead of focusing on the 98 percent of the people who gave you good feedback, you chose to focus on the 2 percent who didn't say anything. Since you didn't get any praise from 2 percent of your colleagues, you make the assumption that your presentation wasn't any good. This then causes you not to participate in any other events.

## 10: Labelling

Labelling is an intense combination of overgeneralization and all or nothing thinking. Instead of describing a certain behaviour, a person who processes their thoughts through labelling, will attach a highly emotive and negative label to themselves or to other people that doesn't leave any room for change.

For example, you are rushing to fill out an application form and hand it in before the deadline. You manage to submit it, but the form is sent back to you because you forgot to include your surname. You then label yourself as stupid because of this one mistake instead of attributing it to the fact that you were rushing so that you wouldn't miss the deadline.

I am assuming that you can recognize your thinking pattern in one or more than one of these cognitive distortions. Before you start panicking, you don't need to, you are at a good place. The fact that you are capable of recognizing your negative thinking patterns means that you are heading in the right direction towards change. Which is what the next chapter is all about.

# Dismantling Toxic Thoughts

## Positive Affirmations

Positive affirmations are an essential technique use in Cognitive Behavioral Therapy. They are used to counteract negative thoughts and beliefs that have been ingrained into the subconscious mind. There is more to an affirmation than repeating words, it is a process of recognizing your negative thoughts and speech, and making a conscious decision to replace them with positive affirmations. The majority of mental illness starts in the mind, which means that if you can change the way you think, you can reverse the condition. No matter who you are, or what position you hold in life, positive affirmations can greatly improve your circumstances if you allow them to work for you.

Do you remember what you read about the subconscious mind at the beginning of the book? When you make the decision to dismantle toxic thoughts, you are reprogramming all of the negative information that has been stored over the years. To those who were emotionally abused as children, every negative word that your parents spoke to you were affirmations that eventually became your reality.

Remember, you are not going to experience change overnight. You are dealing with years of deeply ingrained information that is going to fight to stay. There is going to be a large gap between your perceived inner truth and the positive affirmation, bridging this gap is going to take a significant amount of time. When you start repeating positive affirmations you will experience a strong negative reaction. Firstly, you will feel as if you are lying because nothing about you or your life matches what you are saying. This feeling is an indication that you are on the right track. If you feel a sense of well-being and joy, your mind is immediately responding to something that it knows to be true.

Affirmations transform the way you think and feel about things, once you replace your old negative belief system with a new positive belief system, a change in your behaviour will come easily and naturally.

If you are really serious about overcoming your condition, as soon as you start to repeat positive affirmations you will fall in love with them. If you are ready to start implementing positive affirmations into your life, keep reading.

## How to Create Positive Affirmations

I am going to give you a list of positive affirmations that you can use as a guide, but the most effective way to create affirmations is to create positive affirmations that match your circumstances. Follow these three steps to create your own affirmations:

1. Spend some time thinking about the areas in your life that you want to change, and the ideal life you would like to live now.

2. Get a pen and paper, and write down the areas in your life that you want to change that are most important to you.

3. Next to each point, write a positive statement that is in the present tense. It is important that you focus on what you want and not on what you don't want. For example, if you want to be in a loving relationship, your positive affirmation could be: *"I am in a healthy loving relationship with my ideal partner."*

There are a wide range of affirmations, during the beginning stages of Cognitive Behavioral Therapy, a lot of your affirmations are going to focus on releasing things, basically letting go of everything negative in your life. The reason why many therapists start here is to help you overcome the initial resistance you are going to have towards the process. Here are some positive affirmations that are generally used in Cognitive Behavioral Therapy.

## Releasing Affirmations

- I have released all negative experiences from my past

- I have released the fear of failure

- I have released the fear of not being good enough

- I have released feelings of guilt

- I have released feelings of doubt

- I have released feelings of failure

## Joy Affirmations

- I wake up every morning overflowing with joy in my heart

- I see joy in the lives of everyone that I meet

- I release joy into the lives of everyone that I meet

- People can see joy in my life

## Health Affirmations

- I am fit and healthy

- I live a healthy lifestyle

- My body is in a constant state of healing

- All cells in my body vibrate health and energy

## Love Affirmations

- I am a loveable character

- I give and receive love willingly

- People show me love everyday

- I have got a beautiful partner who loves me for who I am

## Self Esteem Affirmations

- I am more than capable of achieving what I want in life

- I am wonderful and unique

- I love myself for who I am

- I am an amazing person

## Weight Loss Affirmations

- I am my ideal weight

- I am fit and healthy

- I make time to exercise everyday

## How to Use Your Affirmations

Now that you have made your list of affirmations, you have to start incorporating them into your daily life. As mentioned, positive affirmations are not just something that you repeat once a day and then get on with the rest of your day. The idea is to use them to challenge your thinking. Now, I am well aware of the fact that it is virtually impossible to monitor every thought that runs through your mind. What is possible, is to challenge your dominant thoughts. So when you catch yourself thinking something like, "No one likes me," you challenge it with saying, "I am a loveable character," over and over again until the negative thought has left you, and you start to feel more positive about yourself.

- **Morning and Night:** Outside of using your affirmations to challenge your negative thoughts. You want to get into a routine of repeating them on a daily basis. The easiest way to do this is to repeat them as soon as you wake up in the morning and before you go to bed at night.

- **Look in the mirror:** Some of the most impactful messages you have been given, whether positive or negative have been from people looking you directly in the eye. When you look yourself in the eye when you are repeating your affirmations, you are reminding yourself of how important the message is to you.

- **Post it notes:** To remind yourself to keep saying your affirmations, write them on post it notes and stick them in places that you will see them such as your fridge, mirrors, laptop and car windscreen.

- **Say them with passion:** The more emotion you put into repeating your affirmations, the more effective they are. This is a way to trick your mind into believing that what you are saying is true.

- **Chant or Sing Your Affirmations:** If you can take some time out to turn your affirmations into songs the better they will be. Not only does the mind respond better to melodies, it will be easier for you to remember them.

Repeating your affirmations continuously, and with passion will chip away at the most stubborn resistance. Once this resistance has been broken, your subconscious will then be able to re-evaluate your old core beliefs and thinking patterns. This is the main aim of Cognitive Behavioral Therapy. Once your own new inner truths have been established, things in your life will start to change very quickly.

## STOPP

STOPP is another cognitive behavioral technique that will help you to control your negative thoughts and emotions. This is how it works:

**S**top! = Just take a break from whatever you are doing.

**T**ake a breath = pay attention to the way you are breathing.

**O**bserve = What are you thinking about at this very moment?

What are you focusing your attention on?

What is causing you to react the way that you are?

How is your body reacting to what you are thinking about?

**P**ull back = put your thoughts into perspective

- Is there a bigger picture to think about?

- Is there any other way you can look at the situation?

- Look at it from a birds eye view?

- If your friend was in the same situation what advice would you give?

- What would someone you trust say to you right now?

- Is your thought based on fact or opinion?

- Is there another explanation that is more reasonable?

- Is your thought important? Will you attach the same level of importance to it in 6 months time?

- It will pass

**P**ractice what works – move forward

- What is the best thing for you to do right now?

- What is best for you, for others and for the situation?

- Is there anything you can do that lines up with your values?

- Do what will be appropriate and effective

**STOPP – How to Use it**

- For three days, practice the first two steps several times per day.

- Keep reading through the steps to get familiar with them.

- Print the steps out and carry them around with you.

- Practice by going through the steps as many times as you can throughout the day, regardless of whether you need to or not.

- Start using it for little things that upset you.

- As time goes on, you can start to use it for more disturbing situations. It will become like a new habit or skill that becomes an automatic reaction.

**The Steps in Detail**

**Stop!** As soon as you realize that your mind and or your body is reacting to a trigger, say the word "Stop!" The word stop, creates a gap between the trigger and your response. When you are experiencing an attack, use the technique as soon as you possibly can. The earlier you use it, the better it works.

**Take a Breath:** Taking deep and slow breaths will calm you down, and reduce the levels of adrenaline that are causing the physical reaction in your body.

When you focus on your breathing, you take the focus off the negative thoughts and distressing feelings; this process clears the mind and enables you to think more rationally and logically.

**Observe:** You can pay attention to your thinking, to the way your body is reacting and to the desire you have to act impulsively. You are capable of noticing the vicious cycle of anger, sadness, anxiety or depression.

When you realize that you are experiencing these thoughts and feelings, it takes the power away from them. There would be something seriously wrong if you were not aware of how you were thinking and feeling.

**Pull back and put your thoughts into perspective:** This is where you begin to challenge your thoughts, and attempt to think differently.

When you emotionally step back from a situation, it enables you to see the bigger picture which helps you to reduce negative beliefs. This is done by asking yourself questions related to what you are thinking and feeling.

**Practise what works, move forward:** In Cognitive Behavioral Therapy, this is where you learn to change your behavior and start doing things differently. Instead of reacting impulsively, which leads to negative consequences, you can choose a more positive and helpful response.

**Thought Reviewing**

Thought reviewing is a step by step process that helps you to change your thinking. It gives you the opportunity to reflect on what you were thinking after you have thought about it when you are no longer acting out of anger or fear. You are then capable of finding a better way to deal with the situation. You can do a thought review for any situation that happened in the past that you would like to have handled in a better way. Here are the seven steps you will need to assist you in reviewing your thoughts:

**1: The situation:** Give a brief description of the circumstances that led to your distressing feelings.

*Example: I gave the wrong answer during a presentation and I can't stop thinking about how embarrassing it was.*

**2: Initial thought:** What was the first thought that crossed your mind? This was probably an automatic or a subconscious thought that you have had previously.

*Example: I feel like a total failure and that everyone thinks I'm stupid, especially the teacher because I wasn't able to answer the question.*

**3: Think about the consequences:** Why do you think you need to change the way you think? Think about the long and short term consequences if you keep thinking this way. Evaluate the relationship, professional, physical, and psychological consequences if you keep thinking like this.

*Example: If I keep thinking like this I will convince myself that its true and I will never be able to make any progress in life because I won't have the confidence to do so.*

**5: Question your initial thought:** In what ways has this thinking benefited you? Do you have any facts that challenge or support your initial thought? Do you have any strengths that you are ignoring? If someone else that you knew was in the same situation, what advice would you give them?

*Example: When I try and be perfect it overwhelms me, I don't need to be so hard on myself. People who are too serious are boring. I prefer to be around people who are kind to themselves. I have said several things that people have been interested in previously. I don't criticize other people who make mistakes.*

**6: Negative thinking:** Give a brief description of the negative thinking attached to your initial thought. Identify which type of thinking it was, e.g.: all or nothing, labelling etc.

*Example: I was mind reading; I assumed that I knew what my colleagues were thinking.*

**7: Background:** Do you have any recollection of when you first started thinking like this? How far back do these roots go? Are you the only person in your family who thinks like this?

# How to Refocus and Retrain Your Awareness

Changing the way a person thinks is essential to overcoming mental disorders. However, it is equally as important that you are able to refocus and retrain your awareness. Over the past few years, this area of Cognitive Behavioral Therapy has been strongly emphasized. In this chapter I am going to introduce concepts referred to as task concentration and mindfulness. These techniques assist in managing distressing thoughts and using your inner strength to redirect your attention.

## Task Concentration

Becoming skilled at being able to redirect your attention away from yourself (this includes mental images, thoughts, and physical sensations. Instead of focusing on your situation, your attention is directed towards what you are doing and your external environment.

The main aim of task concentration is to pay less attention to what's going on inside you and more attention to what's going on around you. Task concentration can be especially useful when faced with a situation that triggers anxiety. It can help you to offset your tendency to direct your attention to the threat and onto yourself when you are feeling anxious.

As you start to practise task concentration, break the process down into two areas of rehearsal. When you were learning to drive, you started out on small quiet roads. Once you got used to driving, you advanced to the busier roads. Apply the same principle to task concentration. These are the two areas of rehearsal:

1. **Situations that are non threatening:** In a non threatening situation you experience a very limited amount of anxiety. If you suffer from social phobia, you may feel slightly anxious going to the store, or hanging out with family and friends.

2. **Situations that are more challenging:** In these situations you might feel higher levels of anxiety. Such situations might include, travelling on public transport during rush hour traffic, shopping in a busy mall, or going to a party where there are a lot of people you don't know.

As your task concentration skills improve you will slowly progress from stage one to stage two.

## Choosing to Concentrate

The main aim of task concentration exercises is not to reduce the amount of time that you spend concentrating, but to intensify your concentration on various aspects of your external environment. The tasks will vary depending on the situation; some tasks might require you to direct your attention to how a person/people are behaving. You may need to listen intently to what a person is saying during a conversation, or focus on balancing a tray of drinks as you walk through a room full of people.

You might find yourself in a situation where you feel anxious, but there is no task for you to focus on. For example, you might be waiting for a doctor's appointment and the room gets really crowded, when you start to feel anxious you can focus your attention on the things that are surrounding you such as smells, sounds, the way the room has been decorated and paying attention to the other people waiting in the room with you.

As you improve, you will become both environment and task focused instead of focusing on your thoughts and feelings when you feel that you are in a seriously threatening situation.

I am now going to introduce you to some exercises, to give you a better understanding of how focusing your attention on images and sensations limits your ability to process the information that you are surrounded by. The exercises will also show you that it is possible to focus your attention on external task related behaviors. Basically, you are capable of choosing what you focus on when your anxiety, depression or mental illness is triggered.

## Listening Exercise

You will need another person for this exercise; you can either do it with your therapist or a friend.

- Sit back to back with your partner.

- Ask the person to tell you a story that is approximately 2 minutes long.

- As the story is being told, focus on the details.

- Once the story has been told, retell the story back to the person.

- Pay attention to how much you focused on the task of listening to the other person, your environment and the amount of attention that you focused on yourself. Use a mark out of 100 on each area.

- Once you have given your summary, ask your partner to give you feedback on your listening capabilities.

- Repeat the exercise, but this time sit face to face and make direct eye contact with the person who is telling the story.

- While the story is being told, distract yourself every so often by focusing on your sensations and thoughts, and then direct your attention back to the person telling the story.

- Retell the story back to the person and make a note in percentages of how you divided your attention between listening, the environment and yourself.

- Repeat this activity over and over again until you have developed a strong ability to control where you focus your attention.

## Speaking Exercise

- Repeat the same steps as in the listening exercise. However, your focus should now be on making your story as clear as possible to the listener.

- Sit face to face and make direct eye contact with the listener.

- Distract yourself from telling the story by focusing on your thoughts, sensations and feelings, and then switch your attention back to what you are saying and onto the listener. Pay attention to the reactions of the listener and whether they understand what you are saying or not.

- Evaluate your performance by dividing your marks into percentages between yourself, the environment and the task.

## Graded Practice

- For this exercise you are going to write out two lists.

- The first list should contain five situations that you don't find threatening.

- When you are writing down the situation, distract yourself by paying attention to your internal thoughts and sensations.

- Read over the list of situations, and focus your attention on your external environment.

- Write the second list, it should contain ten situations that you find threatening. The list should be written in order of importance, starting from the least and working your way up to the highest.

- Go through the list by intentionally going into the situations and then practising task concentrations. In this way you are practising being able to control your anxiety in real life situations.

## Take a Walk

- Go for a walk in a park and pay attention to what you see, hear, smell and feel.

- For a few minutes, focus your attention on the different things you are surrounded by.

- Start by paying attention to what you are listening to.

- Move on to what you can smell.

- Move on to how your feet feel on the ground.

- You can switch your focus onto different sensations, which can help you to focus your attention onto your external environment.

- The aim of alternating your attention between your five senses is to get you to realize that you are capable of directing your attention to whatever you choose.

- You should then focus your attention on different aspects of the park.

- Do this exercise for a minimum of 20 minutes.

- Allow yourself to really soak in the details of your environment, focus on what catches your attention the most. You may find that you have an interest in plants, birds, water or the smell of woodlands.

- Pay attention to how much more relaxed you feel as you focus on the things you are surrounded by.

## Increasing Your Ability to be Mindful

Mindfulness is a form of meditation that is associated with Zen Buddhism. Over the last few years it has become a popular technique for managing stress, dealing with depression and handling chronic pain. Research has discovered that mindfulness meditation can reduce the reoccurrence of conditions such as depression, anxiety and a host of other emotional problems.

## Capturing The Moment

Capturing the moment that you are in without judging your experience is the main aim of mindfulness. It is a simple but challenging process and starts with the following:

- Focus all your attention on what you are currently experiencing.

- Don't make any judgements about what your senses are picking up.

- Do nothing apart from observe what is taking place in your mind and body. You don't need to evaluate why and what is making you feel this way.

Mindfulness literature discusses how the mind automatically forms judgement about your experiences. Depending on the value you place upon them, you will either label them as good, bad or neutral. You give the majority of your attention to the things that make you feel either good or bad, but it is possible that you ignore neutral things or label them as boring.

Mindfulness meditation encourages you to focus your attention on the present moment without passing judgement. The experience is similar to what happens when a baby experiences the world for the first time, they just take everything in and they don't know how to judge because they don't yet have the capacity to do so.

## Experiment

The next time you meet a friend relative or a co-worker; look at them through a new set of eyes. Forget what you previously knew, thought or the opinions you had about them.

You can try this same exercise regardless of where you are. Just spend time looking at your surroundings with fresh eyes as if this is the first time you are seeing it.

## Allowing Your Thoughts to Float

You can practise your mindfulness skills and use them to help you to deal with negative thoughts and unpleasant physical symptoms. For example, if you suffer from social anxiety, you can use your skills to focus on something else other than your anxious thoughts.

## Watching a Train go by

Imagine a train riding through a station; the train is a representation of your thoughts. Each carriage can be a feeling or thought. Visualize yourself as you watch the train pass you by without getting on it. Accept any fears you may have about what people are thinking about you without trying to engage or suppress them. Watch your fears pass by, as if they were a train riding through a station.

## Standing by The Roadside

This is a different version of the previous exercise you have just done. Imagine you are standing by the side of a road that is reasonably busy. Each vehicle that passes by is a representation of your thoughts and sensations. Just watch as the cars pass you by, don't try and change the direction of the traffic, don't try and catch a ride, just let the cars pass by.

## Learning When Not to Listen to Yourself

One of the main advantages of understanding how your emotions can have an effect on the way you think, is that you become aware of when your thoughts are either unrealistic or unhelpful. Mindfulness teaches you how to connect with your thoughts without judging whether or not they are true or not.

Taking into consideration the fact that when you are emotionally distressed, your negative thoughts are unhelpful and distorted, it only makes sense to allow those thoughts to pass you by. Once you become familiar with the thoughts that you are bombarded with when you are anxious or depressed, it becomes easier for you to let those thoughts go instead of dwelling on them, which is what causes you to feel even more depressed and anxious.

## Moving Swiftly on

This chapter has covered some basic Cognitive Behavioral Therapy skills and techniques that will help you to conquer the negative thinking patterns that lead to depression, anxiety, anger and other mental illnesses. As I am sure you have now realized, this is no easy challenge, if you are serious about being an overcomer you are going to have to put the work in. When you decide not to take medication, or to cut down on your medication, you have to deal with every emotion and thought that you are introduced to. I hope that you feel confident enough to move onto the next chapter of this book which focuses on how to rebuild your life and become the person you know you deserve to be.

# Reaching Forward
# to the Things Ahead

Life is about continuously moving forward. People who suffer from mental illness often state that they feel stuck, minutes turn into hours, days turn into nights, months turn into years and before they know it, five, ten and fifteen years has passed them by, and you haven't achieved anything in life. Taking mental illness out of the equation, the main reason why the majority of people never achieve their life goals is because they don't put any effort into achieving them. Most, if not all people have a vision of their ideal life, whether it's a job, a business or to become famous. Whatever it is, in order to get from vision to reality, you have to formulate a plan. After all, would you go on a major trip if you didn't know how to get to your destination? Whether you use a GPS or you have a map, you will follow something to get there. The same process works with your goals. Now that you have decided to turn your life around, and you feel confident enough to actually make something of yourself, it's time to take practical action, formulate some goals, and then construct a plan for how you are going to get there.

## The Process of Goal Setting

The first step in goal setting is to decide what it is that you want to achieve and then making a commitment to attain it. The idea is to set goals that inspire and motivate you, get them out of your head and down onto paper, when you can look at them instead of just thinking about them, they will become more real to you. You will then need to formulate a plan so that you can reach your goals, and as you achieve certain milestones, cross each one of them off.

When you have the desire to live out your ideal life, goal setting is a powerful tool to get you there. Having a set of goals laid out before you will motivate you to achieve them, it helps you to decide what you want out of life so that you are not living aimlessly, and you have something to focus on. Goal setting also helps you to spot the distractions that will lead you away from what you are trying to achieve.

## Why Set Goals?

Every successful person, whether a business man or an athlete, all set goals. Setting goals provides you with short term motivation and long term vision. It helps you to focus your knowledge, and organize your resources and time so that you can make the most out of your life.

By setting clearly defined and concrete goals, you can measure your achievements and take pride in the fulfilment of them. As you keep reaching these milestones, you will see continuous progress in what you previously might have seen as a pointless endeavour. It will also increase your level of confidence as you start to realize that you are capable of doing much more than you had originally thought.

**Setting Your Personal Goals**

The majority of people assume that goal setting means that you make a few New Year's resolutions and that's it. There is a lot more to the process than this. Are you ready to set some goals? Here are the steps that you will need to follow:

1. **Work Backwards:** This sounds that it makes absolutely no sense. If you ever get the chance to study movie directing you will find that a film director starts the film from the end, and works his way backwards to the beginning. When goal setting, the aim is to start with the end in mind. Therefore, the first thing that you need to do is start with the "Big picture," where do you see yourself ten years from now?

2. **Small Targets:** You will then need to break those goals down into smaller targets that you will need to reach in order to meet your lifetime goals.

3. **Get to Work:** Once you have formulated your plan, your next step is to get to work.

This is why the process of goal setting begins with setting lifetime goals. You then work downwards to the goals you can achieve in the next five years, the next year, the next month, the next week, the next day. This is how the process begins. To give you a better idea of what I'm talking about, let's say that you can see yourself as an established writer with five books under your belt, and a New York Times bestselling author in ten years. This means that you are going to have to write a book, the process of writing a book can seem very daunting considering the fact that the average book is 100,000 words long! Now, it doesn't take a rocket scientist to work out that it's not going to take you ten years to write a book! However, you are not going to become an established author overnight. Let's just say that you set a goal to have your first book written within three years. You can break the book down into chapters, and then pages. For example, you might have 20 chapters each containing 5,000 words. If you write 250 words per day, it should take you approximately two months to write one chapter. This means that it will take you 40 months, which is just over 3 years to write the entire book. When you look at it from this perspective, writing a book doesn't seem so unrealistic. Are you ready to start working on your goals? Keep reading to find out what you need to do to get started.

## Step 1: Setting Your Lifetime Goals

As previously mentioned, when setting personal goals the first step you will need to take is to work out what you want to achieve by a certain age. You don't have to write out everything you want to do until the age of 80, but you should have an idea of what you want to achieve in the next ten years. This will shape your decision making process.

To get you thinking, here are some of the areas that you might want to consider setting goals in:

- **Career:** What are your career goals? Do you want to become a manager? A CEO? Do you want to own your own business?

- **Financial:** How much money do you want to make, and when do you want to have achieved these financial goals? Are your financial goals related to your career goals?

- **Education:** Will you need to get any additional qualifications in order to achieve your goals?

- **Family:** Do you want to get married and have children by a certain age? If so, how do you plan on becoming a good partner and parent to your children? How do you want your extended family to view you?

- **Artistic:** Are you a singer? Song writer? Painter? If you are a singer, maybe your goal is to release your own album. If you are a songwriter, maybe your goal is to write a song for someone famous. If you are a painter, maybe your goal is to have your work featured in one of the top galleries.

- **Physical:** Do you want to lose weight? Build muscle? Maintain a healthy body? How do you plan on achieving your fitness goals?

- **Pleasure:** There should be something in your life that you enjoy doing, if you don't already know, find out what it is and start doing it. One of your pleasures might be to travel, your goal might be to travel the world within the next five years.

- **Public Service:** Would you like to do your part in making the world a better place? If so, how do you plan on achieving this?

These bullet points are simply ideas to get you started, you don't have to have a goal in each area. You may have one goal in each category or two goals in two categories. Whatever you decide on, take some time out to brainstorm and reflect on the goals that you want to achieve. If you find that you have several goals, go through the list and trim it down until you have got a few significant goals that you can focus on.

## Step 2: Establishing Smaller Goals

Once you have detailed your lifetime goals, set smaller goals over five years that will assist you in reaching your lifetime goals.

You will then need to create progressively smaller goals over smaller periods of time, all of which will build up to you reaching your lifetime goals. You will need to create the following:

- A one year plan

- A six month plan

- A one month plan

The next step is to create a to do list for every day of the week. The things that you do on a daily basis, should all help you reach your lifetime goals.

At the beginning stages of your goal setting journey, your goals might be to educate yourself on what you need to do to achieve your goals. This can come in the form of reading, watching videos or even finding a mentor. This will assist you in achieving your goals faster because you will know exactly what you will need to do to get there.

**Staying on Track**

A lack of self discipline is one of the major hindrances that prevent people from achieving their goals. There is no such thing as an easy life. If you ask any successful person how they got where they are today, they will all tell you the same thing. They had to cultivate a habit of discipline. This is where most people fail, a lack of discipline combined with no direction is a recipe for disaster. Having a plan is not the only thing you are going to need. I am sure that there are a lot of people in the world who have a plan but look at it every day and say, "I'll start tomorrow." Ten years down the line, and tomorrow has not come. You don't want to become that person, it will cause your mental illness to resurface as familiar feelings of inadequacy start to take over.

I will tell you what worked for me, having an accountability partner. I had a friend who I sat down with and told him what I was planning on doing. Interestingly enough, he has started on the same journey and so we become each other's accountability partners. This worked really well, we would send each other our to do lists for the day the night before, and at the end of the following day we would call each other and find out what we had both achieved. Some days were better than others, but we kept each other motivated and five years later we have both achieved significant goals. Here are some tips to help you to stay on course:

- Be specific about what you want, don't just write out general goals.

- Set priority goals so that you don't start feeling overwhelmed.

- Keep the smaller goals that you are working on realistic. Again, you don't want to feel overwhelmed,

- Set goals that you know you have control over.

- Make sure your goals are realistic. There is nothing wrong with dreaming big. However, setting a goal such as "I am going to write 20 books in one year" is unrealistic.

- Review your goals, they might change, and you might have more to add to them.

- After you have achieved one goal, add another. You never want to end up in life with no goals.

- Don't beat yourself up if you don't achieve your goals by the deadline that you have set for yourself. Set another deadline and keep pressing on.

- Treat yourself after you have achieved each goal, this will motivate you to continue.

# Ten Attitudes That Promote
# a Healthy Mind

The majority of the friends that I have now have been there for me during my worst moments in life. The depression, when I didn't have the mental strength to get out of bed for days at a time, the attempted suicide. When we get together today, and they experience the new me, I am often asked the same question: "How do you maintain this level of joy?" And my answer is always the same, "Because I choose to." As you have read in previous chapters, happiness is a choice, you can either choose to be happy or you can choose to be miserable. I made the decision to live a life of passion and praise. Yes, I have been through a lot in my life, but there are people who have been through much worse and overcome it. The decision wasn't an easy one; I was comfortable in my misery that was all I knew. I had to make a conscious effort to change the way I thought, to stop dwelling on the negative and play a new song in my mind.

You see, whether we like it or not, life is full of problems. I have often heard people say that when you are coming out of one storm, you are walking into another. It's so true, there is always something negative that you have to deal with. The question is are you going to allow your circumstances to define you, or are you going to decide to be fabulous no matter what you are dealing with? Focusing your attention on negativity, or the people who project it is a waste of time and energy. If I was to sit and lament about the baseless things people have to say, or the problems that I have to go through in life, I would be a very miserable person. I prefer to tackle life with a positive mental attitude that propels me through the dark periods with joy in my heart. Having the right perspective provides you with the ability to enhance every area of your life.

It has even been scientifically proven that people with a positive mindset are not only healthier, but they live longer than pessimists. A study conducted by Yale University found that a positive attitude adds an additional 7.6 years to your life. If you want to continue on the journey that you have started and remain in a perpetual state of happiness, you are going to have to take responsibility and retrain your mind. You might have been introduced to some of these concepts in previous chapters, but they have been repeated to remind you of how important it is to put these things into practice. Here are ten attitudes that promote a healthy mind.

## 1: Find Your Personal Source of Joy

Joy is an absolute necessity to our overall wellbeing. Look deep within and discover what personally makes you happy. What inspires you to keep going, to become a better person, to wake up in the morning? No matter how bad you think your life is, there is something that you are passionate about or you wouldn't be reading this. The only people who are reading this book, and especially the ones who have got to the final chapter, are those who deep down believe that life is worth living.

## 2: Accept Your Individuality

There is no one else on this planet that's got the same DNA as you that has the same finger prints or bone structure as you. You are unique! A lot of the time depression and anxiety comes from comparing yourself to other people, you feel as if you are not good enough, that you don't fit in, you don't fit a certain ideal of beauty. Whatever the case may be, such negative thinking will cause you to remain stuck in life and you will find it very difficult to move forward. Your aim should be to become the best version of yourself, and if you spend time developing yourself, your skills, your talents and your abilities you won't have the time or the energy to compare yourself to other people.

## 3: Volunteer

Until you actually get involved in the struggles of other people, you will continue to believe that you have got the worst problems in the world. There is suffering on every corner, if every capable person was to offer a helping hand, the world would be a better place. Unfortunately this isn't the case, human beings are selfish, they only think about themselves and forget that there are some people who would wish to be in their situation. The easiest way to become a volunteer is to join an organization such as a local church. In most cases you will be able to get involved in feeding the homeless, going to hospitals, or visiting old people. Once you realize that life really isn't that bad, you will start to appreciate what you have.

## 4: Gratitude

Living a life of gratitude is essential to a positive mindset, and living a happy and healthy life. Depressed, anxious and negative people tend to focus on what they don't have. This is what they think about continuously, and it becomes a mantra for their lives. As you have learnt, the more you think about something, the quicker it will manifest in your life. This then leads to a pattern of your circumstances confirming what you believe, and you begin to experience the downward spiral of decline.

Take a pen and paper and write down everything that you are grateful for. If you are convinced that you don't have anything to be thankful for watch some YouTube videos of the poverty in places like India and Africa, where people don't even have the basic necessities in life. You can start by being grateful for the fact that you have got running water, a bed to sleep in and clothes on your back. An attitude of thanksgiving will shift the atmosphere that you live in, and invite a spirit of joy into your life. Write out a gratitude list and carry it with you where ever you go, the moment you feel negative energy creeping in, read your list out loud over and over again until you start to feel positive again.

## 5: Exercise Your Mind

The brain is a muscle, and if it doesn't get any exercise it will become limp and unhealthy just like a body that doesn't exercise. Here are some ways that you can exercise your mind on a daily basis:

- Learn a new word

- Solve a math problem

- Do  a crossword

- Play a memory game

- Read something informative

- Brain training exercises

Remember, everything starts in the mind, it is your most valuable tool. The more you invest in it, the stronger it will become.

## 6: Remember That You Are Not Alone

This journey that you have started is not an easy one. There are going to be days when you just feel like throwing in the towel. At times like this it is important that you reach out to someone, don't try and fight this fight alone. Whether it's an accountability partner, your doctor or your psychiatrist, make sure that you make that phone call when you are feeling like things are getting too much for you.

## 7: Eat a Healthy Diet

The majority of people don't realize how important the mind is, which is why whether knowingly or unknowingly, they abuse it. The assumption is that a healthy diet only has benefits for the body; however, a growing body of evidence points to the fact that it is just as important for the mind. According to the Mental Health Foundation, a good diet is essential to mental health. The foundation also suggests that diet, can play a role in the prevention, management and development of certain conditions including:

- Alzheimer's disease

- Attention deficit hyperactivity disorder (ADHD)

- Depression

- Schizophrenia

There is no suggestion that diet has the ability to control these conditions, neither should patients stop taking medication and embark on a healthy eating regime. However, diet can play a powerful role when combined with other treatment whilst managing these conditions.

The Mental Health Foundation also reports that less than half of those who have been diagnosed with a mental health condition state that they eat fresh fruit on a daily basis. On the other hand, two thirds of people who do not suffer from mental health problems claim that they do eat fresh fruits every day.

The conclusion is that eating a healthy and balanced diet contributes to feelings of well being. A balanced diet is made up of foods that contain the right minerals, vitamins, proteins, carbohydrates and fats, as well as drinking plenty of water.

## 8: Pay attention to what you read, listen to and watch

You will often hear people mention that some books are 'pulp fiction' or 'trash.' What they are referring to are books that are easy to read and don't challenge the mind. Reading books like this every so often are not going to do any harm, just as much as eating a hamburger every once in a while won't affect your health. However, eating junk food everyday is bad for the body in the same way that reading pulp fiction books every day is bad for the mind.

It's worth taking a few moments to think about your mind diet every so often. Ask yourself the following questions:

- How good or bad is your mind diet?

- What are you consuming more of? Books, films, videos that challenge the mind, or reality TV and pulp fiction?

- How is this affecting you as a person?

- Do you need to make any improvements to your mental diet?

If you are finding it difficult to build good mind diet habits, think about someone that you admire, study their habits. Research the kind of books they read and the things that have inspired them to become who they are.

## 9: Surround Yourself With The Right People

It is imperative that you remove all negative people out of your life. This sounds very extreme, but it is essential to your mental health. We have all heard the saying "You can choose your friends but you can't choose your family." This is indeed true, but if you do have negative family members, which you probably will, you are going to have to keep them at arm's length. People fail to realize how much power family members can have over them. You will find that there is a lot of emotional blackmail in families, and it becomes difficult to free yourself from them. If it means that you have to save up some money and move out of home, that is what you are going to have to do. Your emotional stability is more important than a nagging mother who wants you to stay at home so she can have someone to complain to all day!

The same applies with friends, another well known saying is "Misery loves company," or "Birds of a feather flock together." These sayings are very true, groups of friends will tend to have the same mindset, positive people find it difficult to associate with negative people because they drain their energy. There is a high likelihood that the majority of your friends have the same mindset as you. When you get together, everything you talk about is negative, and you never have anything good to say. As difficult as this is going to be, you are going to have to distance yourself from such people, or you will never reach your goals. Such friends will find your new mindset threatening, without meaning to they will say and do things to keep you on the same level as them. If they are not ready to fly with you, you are going to have to say goodbye!

## 10: Enjoy Life

What do you enjoy doing? Do you like to travel? What are your hobbies? When we take part in doing something that we love, we emit positive emotions which will attract the happiness and joy you have been looking for. It might be something as simple as reading a book while soaking in a hot tub, or watching your favorite movies back to back. Whatever it is, make sure that you find time in your schedule to do indulge in it. Remember, you only live once, living a life of misery and sadness isn't worth it. Make a career out of doing what you enjoy and pay attention to how much you flourish when you get to do things that bring you pleasure.

# Conclusion

Congratulations! I'm so glad that you made it to the end of this book. As you have read, there is no quick fix to overcoming mental illness regardless of its nature. This is something that you are going to have to fight for the rest of your life. The good news is that you have now been equipped with the right tools to be able to do so. However, you have to make the choice as to whether you are going to use them or not. The more you practise the exercises in this book, the easier it will become to deal with the many pressures that come with mental illness.

Perseverance, dedication and determination are essential if you want to break free from the constraints of psychological disorders. I am a living testimony that it is possible to do so.

I wish you every success as you continue to travel on your journey to total freedom.

* 9 7 8 1 9 8 5 3 0 0 0 5 7 *